To my husband, Doug.
Thank you for encouraging me to write.

BEAUTIFULLY PREPARED

Restoring the Magnificence of Your Purpose

MONICA SCHAEFER

Illustrations by Julie Headland

Clovercroft Publishing

Beautifully Prepared

© 2016 by Monica Schaefer

All rights reserved. No part of this book may be reproduced or transmitted in any form or by any means, electronic or mechanical, including photocopying, recording or by any information storage and retrieval system, without permission in writing from the copyright owner.

Published by Clovercroft Publishing, Franklin, Tennessee

Published in association with Larry Carpenter of Christian Book Services, LLC.
www.christianbookservices.com

Scripture taken from the NEW AMERICAN STANDARD BIBLE®, Copyright © 1960,1962,1963,1968,1971, 1972,1973,1975,1977,1995 by The Lockman Foundation. Used by permission.

Illustrated by Julie Headland

Cover and Interior Design by Suzanne Lawing

Edited by Gail Fallen

Printed in the United States of America

978-1-942557-36-4

INTRODUCTION

Eve's story holds a key to unlock true beauty in our own lives. Like an ancient, precious work of art whose magnificence has been distorted and obscured by layers of time, Eve's purpose must be uncovered and restored in order for us to behold the truth of her beauty.

The process of restoration begins by understanding Eve's role in the Bible. Eve's life foreshadows the role of the Bride of Jesus* while demonstrating humanity's need for the pure love of God to be embedded deeply within our hearts.

God formed Eve and called her "good." God fashioned Eve for a high calling and purpose: to become one with Adam, to be fruitful and multiply, and to subdue and rule over creation, all in reliance on the goodness of her Creator.

A lie persuaded Eve to believe she was incomplete and called to a different purpose. Once Eve came into agreement with the distortion of truth, she became a slave to the liar . . . as well as the lie.

Eve became her own enemy by believing a lie about the essential truth of her identity. The enmity Eve should have had toward the liar evolved into animosity and hatred against herself. Thus began the distortion of her purpose.

But an opportunity for transformation came in a master restorative plan through the life, death, and resurrection of the Son of God, Jesus. The restorative plan allows the shackles of Eve's bondage to be broken as

---

* The book of Revelation likens followers of Jesus to the image of a bride who has yielded her life to Jesus as her husband. The follower unites with God through Jesus just as Adam and Eve became one flesh in marriage in Genesis 2:24.

she rejects the lies about her purpose. Beautifully prepared, Eve is restored to the truth of her irreplaceable role in creation— perfect union with her Bridegroom.

The liar slithered into my life before I attained four years of age, but I didn't recognize my agreement with the lie until many years later.

My parents bought a large orange grove to transform into barns and pastures suitable for a horse farm. The acquisition meant my two older brothers and I, along with grandparents, uncles, aunts, and various friends, joined my parents during weekends to clear trees, disk soil, and dig postholes. Clearing the land to develop smooth pastures involved walking behind a moving pickup and heaving the debris of wood and rocks into the truck's bed. Even though the work took place under the blazing Florida sun, we children delighted in the funny stories and jokes recounted amongst the older generations as we worked together.

However, we hated one thing about the weekends: the snakes. My dad and brothers would always say, "The only good snake is a dead snake," and I wholeheartedly agreed. One vivid memory involved us pushing the pickup when its battery died. As I focused all my energy toward moving forward, I was shocked to look down between my legs and face a brown coiled snake hissing its tongue at me. I froze, then screamed and leapt away, believing my father would slay the serpent with his trusty "flat-head" shovel while I ran for cover.

The memory of the snake popped into my mind when I considered Genesis 3:15 in my first Bible study fifteen years later. God spoke to the serpent after Adam and Eve had eaten the forbidden fruit, saying,

"And I will put enmity
between you and the woman,
and between your seed and her seed;
He shall bruise you on the head,
and you shall bruise him on the heel."

"Aha," I thought, "therein lies the justification for my hatred of snakes," although I would not see the relationship between Eve and the serpent until much later. Nonetheless, it had a greater influence on my life than I had first considered. I had actually come to the first Bible study at the suggestion of a psychologist, whom I was seeing for relief from feelings of stress, anger, and incompetence. I was almost thirty years old, a new Christian, attractive, and bright, yet entwined in a sexual relationship with a divorced, wealthy older man who was having an affair on me! Thus began my search for freedom from the ugliness of shame and self-hatred. I sought the true beauty of those who knew the peace of God.

Intrigue compelled me to consider the life of Eve, the first woman mentioned in Bible, in contrast with the Bride, the last woman depicted in the Bible. Eve fell into the trap of the liar because she lacked what the Bride possesses: union with God's perfect love or Jesus.

My friend Julie Headland painted a series of portraits capturing glimpses of Eve transforming into the Bride. The images and written reflections in the book testify how true beauty arises through the perfect love of Jesus. The beauty of His love transforms and completes us.

The book calls you to press beyond a profession of faith into a full, transformative relationship of love with God through Jesus. This hurting world needs you—the *best* part of you. "You" restored to your original intent. "You" free of the lies, encumbrances, and entanglements derailing your purpose in life. God beautifully formed and fashioned you with unique attributes and talents to attain a high calling and purpose. Walking in union with Jesus beautifully prepares you to complete your irreplaceable role in creation.

My prayer is for you to break free from the bondage of lies you have believed and to come into the truth so you may restore magnificence to your purpose.

—Monica Schaefer

HOW YOU CAN USE THIS BOOK

Beautifully Prepared is designed so the illustrations give your mind room to ponder the written text at your own pace. Some may read the book entirely at one time, while others might focus on a specific section. The text and illustrations are divided into three sections. Each section can be read independently to afford you the flexibility of keeping the book on a coffee table and considering it over a longer time.

The book's cover comes from one of the portraits in the book, *She Divines in Beauty*. "Beauty" refers to the subject reflecting the glory and peace of Jesus, the source of perfect beauty. One who divines in beauty obtains revelation and understanding as she abides in the presence of God.

My hope is you receive revelation and understanding of your purpose and destiny as you experience the book. You are encouraged to begin reading by asking the Spirit of God to lead you through the message. Ruminate over the text and images with God leading you toward portions relevant to your current situations.

Daily Meditation—You can use the portrait pages as a daily meditation. Each image has been paired with a relevant verse from the Bible and a brief reflection to prompt your personal time with God.

Scripture Meditation—A Scripture meditation at the back of the book contains the initial Scriptures which led me to write *Beautifully Prepared*. These Scriptures may be helpful in launching your own study of Eve in relation to the Bride.

Resources—A resource section at the end of the book provides a list of study and ministry resources.

SECTION ONE:
UNCOVERING THE LIE

Growing up, I didn't have a label for the deceptive scheme and the underlying lie, but I knew how it felt. The hatred, dislike, or distrust of women, known as misogyny, manifests in varying ways, from jokes and pornography to domestic violence, genital mutilation, and honor killings. Misogyny also manifests in abortions, sexual immorality, divorce, addictions, and suicide, when a woman hates herself. The lie of self-hatred whispers that something is fundamentally wrong with us, making us unlovable, unwanted, and worthless.

My childhood was filled with love, and I enjoyed the affection of parents who cherished me. But even the most loved child receives a barrage of messages, many serving as lies when applied as the truth of her identity. Various influences began to cloud and distort the lens I used to understand my role and purpose as a woman. Some messages included marketing from magazines and television; the interchange between significant male and female role models within my family and neighborhood; and community traditions, like an annual parade focused on rewarding women with plastic beads for publicly displaying their breasts; as well as the predatory pornographic industry in my hometown, the reputed strip-club capital of the world.

Lies slowly metastasized to the point where every fiber of my being believed I was unlovable. Feelings of incompetence, hatred, shame, and enmity further contorted and prescribed how I assessed myself. My logic reasoned, "If people knew the truth about me, they will hate me, and I will ultimately be alone." So I learned to perform well and to excel in ways pleasing to the ones I loved the most. I developed a beautiful appearance and a clever wit to allure the eyes of men and to elevate my status among women. I learned legal skills and developed a career to bait the love and respect of my parents. I played all the angles to ensure friends and family members would love me and need me.

None of these wiles comforted the inner fear telling me I would be rejected and alone if I did not control my circumstances. At the age of thirty, I accepted God's free gift of salvation through His Son, Jesus, in the hope of attaining some inner peace. I understood all of my past offenses were forgiven. I learned to sense the presence and direction of the Spirit of God. Yet many of the emotions I felt as a "non-Christian," like anger, fear of failure, rejection, shame, bitterness, and self-hatred, still made guest appearances in this new creation. I continued to walk in self-destructive ways to maintain control over my life's circumstances. Likewise, I remained sexually promiscuous and over-indulgent, desiring material gain, status, and acceptance—just to name a few.

Deep inside, I even believed perhaps biblical principles worked for others but were insufficient to transform the ugliness within me. Even so, I longed to be part of a company described as "the Bride," because God neither rejects nor abandons her. The Bride holds a place of love and acceptance with God, and He unites her with Jesus, His Beloved Son. So, I performed for God. I held Bible studies in the courthouse, I opened my home for worship nights and prayer groups, I facilitated healing ministries, and I resigned my judicial position to serve God as a missionary in the Middle East.

The Spirit of God continued to lead and convict me in many ways. Parts of my journey were genuinely motivated by love for God, but even the good carried the stench of the lie driving me—fear. I ran from situations whenever I feared my incompetence would be exposed, recklessly sabotaging the direction God was leading me. My heart wanted to honor God as I presided over people's lives as a circuit court judge, but during my tenure I was haunted by feelings of incompetence. Now I recognize my decision to resign the position of judge to serve God as a missionary was partially motivated to protect myself from what I feared—the eventual exposure of my incompetence as a judge. Both positions were a great honor, but the good was tainted by the stench of the lie.

In all of my choices, I was seeking more than God's righteousness. I needed to know I was right and everyone else was wrong. Just like Eve, I believed the lie. I ran to eat from the tree of the knowledge of good and evil rather than relying on God to carry me out of the wilderness I was wandering.

Managing the fear left me exhausted, weary, and longing to know a place of true rest and peace within myself. Finally, the time came when I chose complete faith and trust in God, in His character, and in the truth of His promises, because I did not want to run.

COVERED BY LOVE

"Before I formed you in the womb I knew you, And before you were born I consecrated you; I have appointed you a prophet to the nations."
—Jeremiah 1:5

COVERED BY LOVE

The beauty and magnificence of life shine so brightly in young children. The image captures the true beauty of a five-year-old. She delights in the beauty of God's creation and trusts she is complete and good.

You are a precious work designed and equipped for God's purposes. Maybe your purpose has become distorted and obscured with lies. God wants to restore the magnificence of your beauty to you. Likewise, this hurting world needs to experience your true beauty.

Do you have a photo of yourself at age four or five? Take time to examine it. Ask God to reveal the true purposes He consecrated you to accomplish. Open your heart to experience His restoration.

SHE WEDS IN BEAUTY

"Then I heard something like the voice of a great multitude and like the sound of many waters and like the sound of mighty peals of thunder, saying, 'Hallelujah! For the Lord our God, the Almighty, reigns. 'Let us rejoice and be glad and give the glory to Him, for the marriage of the Lamb has come and His bride has made herself ready.' It was given to her to clothe herself in fine linen, bright and clean; for the fine linen is the righteous acts of the saints."

—Revelation 19:6–8

SHE WEDS IN BEAUTY

The Book of Revelation presents a letter from the apostle John to seven churches, containing prophecy of future events written in an apocalyptic style. The style employs imagery and symbolism to convey a message. For example, chapters 19 and 20 depict Jesus as the Lamb of God and His followers as "the Bride of the Lamb."

This portrait, in sequence with *They Unite in Beauty* and *She Reigns in Beauty*, illustrates Eve transformed into the Bride. Here, all of heaven rejoices with gladness when one person overcomes the liar's authority by surrendering her heart to the love of Jesus and her walk to the lead of His Spirit.

The Scripture gives me pause to ponder the spiritual battle over each of our lives if such a celebration occurs at the victory over the liar. The apostle Paul encouraged the Ephesians to put on the full armor of God in order to stand firm against the schemes of the devil, because our struggle is not against flesh and blood, but against the spiritual forces of wickedness in the heavenly places. The Bride makes herself ready, united with the one to whom all authority on heaven and earth has been given, Jesus (Matt. 28:18; Eph. 1:20–22).

Will you give cause for celebration in heaven today? Ask God to lead you in making yourself ready.

THEY UNITE IN BEAUTY

"Blessed are those who are invited to the marriage supper of the Lamb."
—Revelation 19:9

THEY UNITE IN BEAUTY

The portrait demonstrates perfect beauty emanating from your union with the love of Jesus. Union comes at the point of our full surrender to God's leading over our lives. Specifically, the point when we lay down everything, including our expectations of God, and surrender the direction and outcome of our lives to God. Experiencing His great love and forgiveness draws us to follow His lead.

We no longer struggle for independence but abide in submission to our Beloved. The union blesses all who experience the Bride's testimony and all who witness her life in union with Jesus.

Consider the price of full surrender. Are you willing to make Him Lord and Master of your whole life? Ask God to reveal any entanglements restraining you from full surrender to His lead.

SHE REIGNS IN BEAUTY

"Then I saw thrones, and they sat on them, and judgment was given to them. And I saw the souls of those who had been beheaded because of their testimony of Jesus and because of the word of God, and those who had not worshiped the beast or his image, and had not received the mark on their forehead and on their hand; and they came to life and reigned with Christ for a thousand years.

"Blessed and holy is the one who has a part in the first resurrection; over these the second death has no power, but they will be priests of God and of Christ and will reign with Him for a thousand years."

—Revelation 20:4, 6

SHE REIGNS IN BEAUTY

The "thousand years" can symbolically depict an age rather than a literal period of time in the future. As used here, the number represents the current church age, a period from the resurrection of Jesus through His final return and judgment of humanity.

The Scripture portrays some characteristics of the Bride describing one who has been beautifully prepared to reign with Jesus:

1. She relinquished self-governance to the point of persecution, represented as one who has been beheaded. In other words, she presents her life to God to accomplish His purposes (Rom. 12:1).
2. She reflects the image of her Bridegroom and manifests the spiritual authority of God's love (1 John 4:16–18).
3. She unites with God through Jesus and obtains the first resurrection when she is born of the Spirit of God. Physical death has no sting for her (John 3:5, 5:25–28).

The portrait and Scriptures describe the position we are called to occupy. By occupying the position of the Bride, you complete the restoration of Eve, reigning over creation with the Bridegroom.

SHE WARNS IN BEAUTY

"After these things I saw another angel coming down from heaven, having great authority, and the earth was illumined with his glory. And he cried out with a mighty voice, saying, 'Fallen, fallen is Babylon the great! She has become a dwelling place of demons and a prison of every unclean spirit, and a prison of every unclean and hateful bird. For all the nations have drunk of the wine of the passion of her immorality, and the kings of the earth have committed acts of immorality with her, and the merchants of the earth have become rich by the wealth of her sensuality.'

"I heard another voice from heaven, saying, 'Come out of her, my people, so that you will not participate in her sins and receive of her plagues; for her sins have piled up as high as heaven, and God has remembered her iniquities.'"

—Revelation 18:1–5

SHE WARNS IN BEAUTY

We are called to come out of the ways of harlotry, represented as Babylon, and to become the faithful Bride, singularly focused on following the lead of Jesus. The liar aims to enslave us to self-focused ways, leading to death and destruction. We must choose whom we will serve and stop playing the harlot.

A cup of great sorrow awaits those who cling to self-governance. God is calling us to come out of old ways and to unite with Him. Jesus warned us in Matthew 7:21, *"Not everyone who says to Me, 'Lord, Lord,' will enter the kingdom of heaven, but he who does the will of My Father who is in heaven will enter."* God calls the Bride to live distinguishable from the ways of the world (Mark 9:47; 1 Cor. 6:9–10; Eph. 5:5; 1 John 3:9).

The Bride recognizes from where she has come. All of her being desires to be set apart unto her Bridegroom. Compelled by His love, she warns others of the schemes of the liar. She truthfully testifies of the darkness of bondage to the lie. Simultaneously, she lovingly calls all to the abundant life of union with the love of Jesus.

Spend some time with God. Ask Him to show you whether you are clinging to self-governance rather than to reliance upon Him.

SHE THRIVES IN BEAUTY

"Now as they were traveling along, He entered a village; and a woman named Martha welcomed Him into her home. She had a sister called Mary, who was seated at the Lord's feet, listening to His word. But Martha was distracted with all her preparations; and she came up to Him and said, 'Lord, do You not care that my sister has left me to do all the serving alone? Then tell her to help me.' But the Lord answered and said to her, 'Martha, Martha, you are worried and bothered about so many things; but only one thing is necessary, for Mary has chosen the good part, which shall not be taken away from her.'"

—Luke 10:38–42

SHE THRIVES IN BEAUTY

God designed us to flourish in the presence of His Love. Our works fueled by any other source will eventually lead to failure. You and I can only achieve our high calling and purposes in union with Jesus.

How do we know if we are fueled by something other than God? God leads us gently and tenderly. Every other motivation drives us . . . like a slave.

The apostle Paul helps us discover our true motivation in Galatians 5:19–23. When we find ourselves in situations characterized with the following, then something other than the spirit of God is leading our participation: enmity, strife, jealousy, immorality, drunkenness, outbursts of anger, disputes, or dissensions. In contrast, circumstances motivated by God bring about love, joy, peace, patience, kindness, goodness, faithfulness, gentleness, and self-control.

God desires to lead you so you thrive. Spend some time with God, asking Him to show you the true motivation of your heart. Is a lie stealing your peace?

SHE TRADES IN BEAUTY

"And he [the beast] causes all, the small and the great, and the rich and the poor, and the free men and the slaves, to be given a mark on their right hand or on their forehead, and he provides that no one will be able to buy or to sell, except the one who has the mark, either the name of the beast or the number of his name."

—Revelation 13:16–17 (brackets mine)

[In all of my choices, I was seeking more than God's righteousness. I needed to know I was right and everyone else was wrong. Just like Eve, I believed the lie. I ran to eat from the tree of the knowledge of good and evil rather than relying on God to carry me out of the wilderness I was wandering.

Managing the fear left me exhausted, weary, and longing to know a place of true rest and peace within myself. Finally, the time came when I chose complete faith and trust in God, in His character, and in the truth of His promises, because I did not want to run.]

[Finally, the time came when I chose complete faith and trust in God, in His character, and in the truth of His promises.]

SHE RESTS IN BEAUTY

The portrait and Scripture depict the essence of the new way we must walk, resting and relying on the goodness of God's love. Experiencing the goodness of His nature and the depth of His love feeds our faith and our trust in Him. We experience the perfect sustenance of His love, even at our darkest hour, as we walk, leaning on Him.

Can you recall a time you experienced the goodness of God's nature?

Jesus is your rest. He said, *"Come to Me, all who are weary and heavy-laden, and I will give you rest"* (Matt. 11:28).

Are you are in the midst of a dark hour? Spend some time reflecting and asking God to show you His love.

SECTION TWO:
CONFRONTING THE LIE

Like all marriages, mine had conflict. The difference for me was I had no real skills to address our discord since I was most comfortable running from difficult circumstances. God threw a curve ball into my life with the birth of a beautiful baby girl. My love for her would not let me run from the conflict. Staying compelled me to face my fear.

Consequently, I partnered with the Spirit of God, who faithfully led me and taught me how to apply the gift of salvation to the angry and rebellious areas of my nature. Then I could truly love my own self, my husband, and others. My role in the partnership was to wait attentively for the leading of the LORD. The waiting taught me humility, honesty, and openness before the Spirit of God, making room for true repentance and transformation.

A prayer posture of humility—my head low to the ground and my heart bowing to the sovereignty of God—led me to relinquish my pride. Surrendering my pride meant giving up my need to run, to always be right, to control the outcome of every situation, or to have things go my way. Pride dissipated as I stayed to face the hard situations, as I saw my culpability, as I admitted I did not have the solution for every situation, and as I released the circumstances from the grip of my control.

An honest assessment of my conduct brought forth genuine feelings of sorrow, allowing me to clearly identify and to speak the feelings and repentance to God, as well as to those whom I had injured.

Opening my heart to receive truth, forgiveness, and its substantial transformation was the final step. My circumstances began to change.

Each encounter with the love and goodness of God fortified my courage and focused my vision so I could see the essential lie about my identity. Eventually, in the prayerful waiting, the Spirit of God led me to the moment I came into agreement with the lie of misogyny. I was only four years old when I began hating myself.

The revelation of truth was an extremely painful experience of anguish and mourning. My heart burned with anguish over the heartache, rejection, and pain I had inflicted on myself, on God, and on many others. Then tears of mourning gushed for the loss of years and opportunities. Simultaneously, a flood of God's love and freedom flowed into my being, along with an open doorway for greater transformation.

Shortcomings remain in my character, and the transformation of my heart has not removed me from difficult situations. However, a true change has taken place within me. The difference can be found in the motivation of my heart. No longer driven by fear but compelled by the fullness of God's love, I face life's challenges without plotting my own course. My heart desires to remain yielded to God, abiding in His presence.

SHE RULES IN BEAUTY

"And she gave birth to a son, a male child, who is to rule all the nations with a rod of iron; and her child was caught up to God and to His throne."

—Revelation 12:5

SHE RULES IN BEAUTY

Chapter 12 of Revelation describes a woman giving birth to a child, as a dragon awaits to devour the newborn. The child is safely caught up to God, to rule all the nations with an iron rod. Some interpretations consider the woman to be representative of faithful followers of God within Israel at Jesus' birth; the child is thought to be Jesus. Others understand the woman to be today's faithful followers of Jesus and the child to be the Bride.

The dragon is identified within the text as "the serpent of old who is called the devil and Satan, who deceives the whole world."

The serpent retains the same job description throughout the entire Bible from Genesis to Revelation: to deceive the whole world. The Bride overcomes the serpent by following the path forged by the Bridegroom, Jesus.

The ones who have overcome the liar are granted access to sit with Jesus on His throne and rule with Him. We spiritually rule with Jesus every time we reject self-governance and walk in submission to God's lead. Each God-led step manifests the glory, sovereignty, and authority of God on Earth.

Facing the fears, examining my contribution to conflicts in my marriage, pressing forward toward truth, and relying on the goodness and leading of the Spirit of God were moments I reflected the message of the portrait.

You, too, can trust in the goodness of God and obey His lead.

Spend some time pondering the image and Scripture. Ask God to show you areas you may be holding onto self-governance rather than His lead.

SHE WAITS IN BEAUTY

"Then the kingdom of heaven will be comparable to ten virgins, who took their lamps and went out to meet the bridegroom. Five of them were foolish, and five were prudent. For when the foolish took their lamps, they took no oil with them, but the prudent took oil in flasks along with their lamps. Now while the bridegroom was delaying, they all got drowsy and began to sleep. But at midnight there was a shout, 'Behold, the bridegroom! Come out to meet him.' Then all those virgins rose and trimmed their lamps. The foolish said to the prudent, 'Give us some of your oil, for our lamps are going out.' But the prudent answered, 'No, there will not be enough for us and you too; go instead to the dealers and buy some for yourselves.' And while they were going away to make the purchase, the bridegroom came, and those who were ready went in with him to the wedding feast; and the door was shut. Later the other virgins also came, saying, 'Lord, lord, open up for us.' But he answered, 'Truly I say to you, I do not know you.' Be on the alert then, for you do not know the day nor the hour."

—Matthew 25:1–13

SHE WAITS IN BEAUTY

You and I will face times when we don't know how to lean on Jesus. These times are when we wait, attentively, like the prudent virgins, abiding in the presence of the Spirit of God.

Jesus promised He would neither abandon nor leave us as orphans. Jesus left us a Helper, God's Spirit of truth (John 14:16–18).

Are you waiting for God to move in your situation? Spend some time with God and ask for Him to reveal His Spirit to you.

SHE SPEAKS IN BEAUTY

"And they overcame him because of the blood of the Lamb and because of the word of their testimony, and they did not love their life even when faced with death."

—Revelation 12:11

SHE SPEAKS IN BEAUTY

Do you feel the power relayed in the Scripture and the painting? *"Death and life are in the power of the tongue, and those who love it will eat its fruit"* (Prov. 18:21).

Fear commandeers your tongue for its power. A heart gripped with lies is bound and restrained from speaking the truth. Jesus died and rose again to set our hearts free. The power of Jesus' resurrection enables us to speak the truth of our heart.

Once our heart experiences freedom through Jesus, we no longer want to live a self-governed life. The apostle Paul wrote in Galatians 2:20, "it is no longer I who live, but Christ lives in me." We overcome the liar—the one falsely accusing us—as we yield our hearts to the sovereignty of Jesus, relinquish our selfish conduct, and speak of the truth within us.

God wants to restore your heart and your tongue. Your voice is important, and the words you say have power. Don't let the liar commandeer your power.

Do you have difficulty speaking the truth of your heart? Spend some time with God, and ask the Spirit of God to show you any areas of your heart bound to a lie. When you recognize a lie, use the power of your tongue to confess the lie as a deception. You can also use your tongue to reject the lie and to come out of agreement with the lie. God's forgiveness and truth will flood you with His love and freedom.

SHE DIVINES IN BEAUTY

"And there was a woman in the city who was a sinner; and when she learned that He [Jesus] was reclining at the table in the Pharisee's house, she brought an alabaster vial of perfume, and standing behind Him at His feet, weeping, she began to wet His feet with her tears, and kept wiping them with the hair of her head, and kissing His feet and anointing them with the perfume."

—Luke 7:37–38 (brackets mine)

SHE DIVINES IN BEAUTY

The imagery of the woman pouring out extravagant worship flooded my mind as I cried over the loss of years and opportunities arising from my agreement with the lie of self-hatred. A heart poured out to God is a truly extravagant form of worship. Extravagant worship opens our heart to experience more of His love.

Have you experienced anguish, sorrow, shame, loss, or pain to the point you are unable to share with another? You can share now. Find a private space to meet with God. He wants to take the weight of those tears from you. Invite Him to show you the way.

SECTION THREE:
PASODOBLE

The Bible begins with the first woman, Eve, who was joined with Adam to subdue and rule over all of creation. The Bible ends with the imagery of a woman, the Bride, who unites with the last Adam, Jesus, to rule and reign over all of creation. The serpent tries to destroy both Eve and the Bride.

The Bride completes Eve's original commission while resting in the perfect love of God. Eve lacked the underpinning of perfect love, so her trust in the goodness of her Creator wavered. Without complete trust in God's leading, Eve opened her heart to the lie. Eve received a life of self-governance when she chose the innate ability to judge good from evil apart from God.

Jesus embodied the perfect love of God. When Jesus came, He surrendered all pride and refused to live by choices independent of God's leading. He only did what His Father showed Him to do, because He and the Father are one. The Bride walks in loving union with God, following the ways of Jesus.

The Bride's union with God reminds me of a beautiful Spanish dance known as the

Pasodoble, which I enjoyed at weddings during my childhood. The individual pairs of dancers in the musical vignette recreate a bullfighter's final pass around a bullfight ring. All the couples flow together to encircle the perimeter of the dance floor, creating a dance within a dance.

A male dancer leads each pair and portrays the matador, while the female partner dances the role of his red cape. The sway and movement of her body gives beauty to the dance. But the cape does not plot out the dance steps; in fact, her most beautiful moves are an extension of the matador's arm when he places her precisely to lure the bull to its defeat.

Older couples were always the most graceful dancers to observe. The effortless union of the firm and skilled matador matched with the surrendered beauty and grace of the cape carries them around the dance floor, enticing young observers to learn and join the dance.

The Bride's true beauty blossoms when she moves as the Matador's red cape. She trusts and relies on God's hand to strategically and beautifully lead her through every twist and turn, while He lures and slays the opposing beast for His kingdom's purposes.

The Bride is comprised of individuals who place their trust in Jesus and surrender their steps to His lead. The Bride is grafted into His royal bloodline. This position, along with God's perfect love, gives the Bride the courage to reject the lie, accept the truth, and yield to God as He crushes the liar's authority over her.

The portrait series invites you and me to join the dance as the Bride. The paintings illustrate the shackles of the lie breaking as we unite with the perfect love of God, receive a transformed heart, and walk as Jesus modeled. Thus, we are beautifully prepared for our irreplaceable role in creation as the Bride, perfectly united with God, completing the restoration of Eve's original intent.

PASODOBLE

"Father, if You are willing, remove this cup from Me; yet not My will, but Yours be done."
—Luke 22:42

[The Bride's true beauty releases when she moves as the Matador's red cape. She trusts and relies on God's hand to strategically and beautifully lead her through every twist and turn, while He lures and slays the opposing beast for His kingdom's purposes.]

PASODOBLE

    The painting and Scripture sum up the restoration of Eve to her original intent, the depiction of the Bride. You and I are restored as we yield to the lead of our Savior, Jesus, even unto death of our own desires. His love completes and transforms Eve, you, and me so we flow as one with Him, never giving ground to the voice of deception.
    Jesus has the highest calling of reconciling all things in heaven and earth unto God the Father (see Col. 1:19–20). Will you unite with the Bridegroom, Jesus, and join Him as He rules over creation in completion of His call?

SHE OVERCOMES IN BEAUTY

"Those whom I love, I reprove and discipline; therefore be zealous and repent. Behold, I stand at the door and knock; if anyone hears My voice and opens the door, I will come in to him and will dine with him, and he with Me. He who overcomes, I will grant to him to sit down with Me on My throne, as I also overcame and sat down with My Father on His throne."

—Revelation 3:19–21

SHE OVERCOMES IN BEAUTY

You do not have to remain in bondage to lies. God knocks on the door of your heart for you to turn to Him. He forged the path for you to overcome the liar. To "be zealous and repent" means you seize the moment, right now, to consider the conduct you regret.

You cease justifying or excusing your conduct. You refrain from blaming others for your ways. If no conduct comes to mind, you reflect on whether or not you have engaged in any conduct enumerated in Galatians 5:19, such as anger, jealousy, immorality, or drunkenness.

Take a deep breath and make space in your emotions to feel the sorrow and regret resulting from your actions.

Speak your sorrow to God.

Ask God to forgive you.

He will respond with His forgiveness.

You, too, will walk a different way, as the Bride, in union with the Lamb of God.

RESTORED IN MAGNIFICENCE

"Therefore if anyone is in Christ, he is a new creature; the old things passed away; behold, new things have come."
—2 Corinthians 5:17

RESTORED IN MAGNIFICENCE

Jesus is magnificence. He sits over all the heavens and the earth. He reigns over all. *"Thine, O Lord, is magnificence, and power, and glory, and victory: and to thee is praise: for all that is in heaven, and in earth, is thine: thine is the kingdom, O Lord, and thou art above all princes"* (1 Chron. 29:11, Douay-Rheims Bible).

Jesus is the Word of God, and, apart from Him, you would not have come into being. *"In the beginning was the Word, and the Word was with God, and the Word was God. All things came into being through Him, and apart from Him nothing came into being that has come into being"* (John 1:1–3).

Jesus knows all about you, including your pain and your needs. He is the only way to complete your needs.

The first time my daughter saw the portrait, she asked if it was an image of me as a child. The portrait represents the transformation I have experienced. I remained in bondage to a lie for over forty years, but once I faced the fear and the lie, the powerful love of Jesus reached through time and renewed my heart to the condition of the intact, purposed-filled heart created while in my mother's womb. His magnificence redeemed the years. The memories are no longer painful, and peace occupies the formerly wounded areas.

The image, the Scripture, and my life testify of a life-saving love embodied in Jesus. God intends for you to unite with Jesus and to reign with Him in magnificence, power, glory, and victory. The hour of your restoration has arrived! Your participation is essential to complete the dance. You are beautifully prepared!

SCRIPTURE MEDITATION

"God created man in His own image, in the image of God He created him; male and female He created them. God blessed them; and God said to them, 'Be fruitful and multiply, and fill the earth, and subdue it; and rule over the fish of the sea and over the birds of the sky and over every living thing that moves on the earth.' Then God said, 'Behold, I have given you every plant yielding seed that is on the surface of all the earth, and every tree which has fruit yielding seed; it shall be food for you; and to every beast of the earth and to every bird of the sky and to every thing that moves on the earth which has life, I have given every green plant for food'; and it was so. God saw all that He had made, and behold, it was very good. And there was evening and there was morning, the sixth day" (Gen. 1:27–31).

"Then the Lord God took the man and put him into the garden of Eden to cultivate it and keep it. The Lord God commanded the man, saying, 'From any tree of the garden you may eat freely; but from the tree of the knowledge of good and evil you shall not eat, for in the day that you eat from it you will surely die'" (Gen. 2:15–17).

"Now the serpent was more crafty than any beast of the field which the Lord God had made. And he said to the woman, 'Indeed, has God said, "You shall not eat from any tree of the garden"?' The woman said to the serpent, 'From the fruit of the trees of the garden we may eat; but from the fruit of the tree which is in the *middle of the garden, God has said, "You shall not eat from it or touch it, or you will die."' The serpent said to the woman, 'You surely will not die! For God knows that in the day you eat from it your eyes will be opened, and you will be like God, knowing good and evil.' When the woman saw that the tree was good for food, and that it was a delight to the eyes, and that the tree was desirable to make one wise, she took from its fruit and ate; and she gave also to her husband with her, and he ate"* (Gen. 3:1–6).

"Do you not know that when you present yourselves to someone as slaves for obedience, you are slaves of the one whom you obey, either of sin resulting in death, or of obedience resulting in righteousness?" (Rom. 6:16).

"The Lord God said to the serpent,
    'Because you have done this,
    Cursed are you more than all cattle,
    And more than every beast of the field;
    On your belly you will go,
    And dust you will eat
    All the days of your life;
    And I will put enmity
    Between you and the woman,
    And between your seed and her seed;
    He shall bruise you on the head,
    And you shall bruise him on the heel.'" (Gen. 3:14–15).

"A great sign appeared in heaven: a woman clothed with the sun, and the moon under her feet, and on her head a crown of twelve stars; and she was with child; and she cried out, being in labor and in pain to give birth.

"Then another sign appeared in heaven: and behold, a great red dragon having seven heads and ten horns, and on his heads were seven diadems. And his tail swept away a third of the stars of heaven and threw them to the earth. And the dragon stood before the woman who was about to give birth, so that when she gave birth he might devour her child.

"And she gave birth to a son, a male child, who is to rule all the nations with a rod of iron; and her child was caught up to God and to His throne. Then the woman fled into the wilderness where she had a place prepared by God, so that there she would be nourished for one thousand two hundred and sixty days" (Rev. 12:1–6).

"He who overcomes I will grant to sit down with Me on My throne, as I also overcame and sat down with My Father on His throne" (Rev. 3:21).

RESOURCES

I recommend the following books should you want to launch into further study on Eve, the Bride, or restoration from a lie:

1. John and Stasi Eldredge, *Captivating: Unveiling the Mystery of a Woman's Soul* (Nashville, TN: Thomas Nelson, 2010).

2. Steve Gregg, *Revelation: Four Views, A Parallel Commentary* (Nashville, TN: Thomas Nelson, 2013).

3. Joseph Herrin, *God's Plan of the Ages* (Montezuma, GA: Heart4God Publishing, 2011), http://www.heart4god.ws/index_htm_files/Gods%20Plan%20of%20the%20Ages.pdf.

4. John Loren and Paula Sandford, *The Transformation Series* (Lake Mary, FL: Charisma House, 2008).

"These will wage war against the Lamb, and the Lamb will overcome them, because He is Lord of lords and King of kings, and those who are with Him are called and chosen and faithful."

—Revelation 17:14